Highway of Poems

by Terrance Merritt

DORRANCE
PUBLISHING CO
EST. 1920
PITTSBURGH, PENNSYLVANIA 15238

Dorrance Publishing Co
585 Alpha Drive
Suite 103
Pittsburgh, PA 15238
Visit our website at *www.dorrancebookstore.com*

ISBN: 979-8-88729-443-8
eISBN: 979-8-88729-943-3

COLORED ST.

DINNER WITH GREATNESS

The table is set for an incredible evening. As I took my seat, Martin Luther asked to pass him the greens. He looked at me and said, "They thought they killed my dream, but it stills lives on in people like you."

Fredrick Douglass interrupted, "Martin, not at the dinner table."

"But you're right," said Tupac as he poured a glass of Alize.

"He must learn that anger is not strength; it's a weakness," replied Fredrick.

Then Kobe leaned in and whispered, "Mamba mentality." Gigi could only roll her eyes because she knows her father's competitive nature still burns.

Langston Hughes asked, "So you're from the same place as Thomas T. Fortune, huh?" Before I could answer, we overheard Brother Muhammad and Brother Malcolm bickering over who was the greatest.

Then out of the blue, Jackie Robinson yelled out, "How 'bout them Dodgers!" The whole room burst out in laughter. Harriet Tubman, in her momma voice, told everyone to quiet down. Then Huey walked in with a shameful look because of what he'd become. But all brothers welcomed him with loving, open arms. As George Washington Carver was about to serve his peanut sandwiches for dessert, Jesus seated at the head of the table stood and made a toast.

"Never fear, my son. We are all in you, and yes, this includes me. Leave your mark on this world and take your place amongst this courageous family tree."

THE BLACK MAN'S PLIGHT

Growing up black I looked up to rappers and hustlers with impunity. Never paying attention to the true pillars of the community. When I leave my home, I'm hunted like an animal. Making me feel less then human. I guess my life has no value; that's what I keep assuming. On the contrary, black lives matter, all lives matter. The politicians and media keep us at odds. So many of us grew up without a father in the home. Before we can read or write our daddies are gone. Mama was there to pick up the pieces. I've witnessed loved ones get incarcerated. Seeing our heroes getting assassinated was the norm in my neighborhood. You can't understand the pain that's growing in my brain. When you elevate your thinking, but no one notices the change. I must ask the question: "What's wrong with the black man speaking with knowledge? What's wrong with intelligence or living with elegance?" Something wrong with our culture?" It's oh so evident. I know, I know, you think I'm being naive. I made a vow to God that I wouldn't mislead. My child or anyone else's down a path of destruction. Holding on to hope while in the grasp of injustice. We're born with scars passed down from slavery. All who gave there life to incredible acts of bravery. Above all else my dignity I hold with the utmost esteem. I'm terrified of being ignorant. So whenever you view me, whether you think I'm wrong or right. Now you understand this BLACK MAN'S PLIGHT.

MEANING

What's the meaning of having it all when you crushed everybody on your way there? It's lonely at the top, huh? Tell me the meaning of hating the next because he or she found the willpower to take a different path. What's the reasoning of being holy when you treat everyone like scum of the earth? It's a just question. What's the thinking behind trying to prove to everyone you're not the person you used to be? You owe this world nothing. What's the mind frame behind shooting someone over the color of their skin, religious background, or sexual preference? It's truly heartbreaking. There is no excuse for any man or woman to neglect their offspring, the most precious thing in life. Enlighten me on why are we taking these penitentiary chances knowing the system designed for us to fail? I've searched and searched deep in my mind I still can't find the meaning.

BRUTALLY HONEST

It's been an age-old struggle from within. We hate each other with no explanation. The slave mentality minus the plantation. Our minds are tedious. Oppressed for centuries. I ask myself are we our biggest enemy? Our history lost. The future bleak. The cycle must be broken. We must reassess and tweak. We should expect our kids to go to college. We should strive to buy a home. The prison system's filled with niggas. While the honest black man outnumbered in corporate America. Imagine if we all stuck together; it would cause mass hysteria.

IMPORTANTS

I see you styling, finessing, getting that bag. But just remember their objective is to trick you off the streets. So I hope you remember what's important to you.

They gas you up; you give them a show. In the same breath they applaud your demise. I been in your shoes. But don't take my word for it. You need to keep an eye on what's important to you.

You work making minimum wage. You refuse to sell your soul for a quick check. The money in your pocket or social status has nothing to do with your value as a human. Keep focusing on what's important to you.

I wake up to go work not because I want to. My children and my family need me. They speak foul words against me, knocking me down. But I get back up stronger than before because I know what's important to me.

CRIES FROM THE SLUMS

We've fought our whole life trying to overcome poverty, violence, and racism. While on a constant chase for the root of all evil. Don't look down upon us; uplift us. Encourage us to a better life. Instill in us hope. We're surrounded by evil. Suffocated by negativity. Loss after constantly seeking the pinnacle of life. We've all played a role in this. The night's terrifying victimized by a culture we created. Incorporated through subliminal messages. Stabilized by an unjust society. We praise this lifestyle. In that lies the irony.

KEEP YOUR SOUL

Your eyes light up with temptation. It's so hard to ignore the allure. Your whole life you dreamed of being a neighbor dope boy. You turn on the television you see extravagant homes, a sporty Tesla, beautiful yachts, with the supermodel wife to match. I suppose this is the American dream we strive for. At what cost? How far are you willing to go? In the end, is it worth it? Are you willing to work hard? Are you just gonna take shortcuts, making shady deals ensuring your wealth. Violently taking from others. That blood money is cursed. The dope money won't last. Ask yourself this: Are you willing to give back? Not buying turkey's for Thanksgiving or presents for Christmas. I mean opening places of business to give them a way to make their own money. Be the example. Keep striving for better but never, ever fold. Temptation will be many; don't let them take your soul.

FAITH AVE.

THEY POISONED THE WELL

As the world becomes engulfed in pestilence, it's the first sign that the enemy has made his move. Humans have opened the door willingly. Not knowing the consequences of our actions.

Right under our noses they've poisoned the future. Faith will be tested will be persecuted. Fear has left us weak, seeking answers. Our God will deliver us. It's the only way.

Don't be afraid to pray, don't be afraid to say that he's the light and always be the way.

THE TEST

A man was awakened from his slumber to knock at the door. "May I asked who knocked at my door?"

"I'm a man bearing gifts, nothing less nothing more. I've scoured the world for someone who's worthy."

"I'm but a peasant, a humble servant. Surely, I'm not worthy."

"Your humble heart proves you are. Even in darkness you remained a star. I'll give you immortality, vast riches, or the power to destroy your enemies. But you can only choose one. You must make your decision before the rise of the sun."

Without a moment's hesitation he replied, "Neither. I already have gifts. I have family and a God who loves me. The money and immortality on earth corrupts the soul."

The stranger could only smile as he vanished into the cold.

INTO THE STORM

As the winds fast approach. The clouds become darker; the silence becomes deafening. Shelter's so close, but the downpour eases my pain. A thought to run this storm is overbearing. The thunder roars like a lion, but yet I find myself calm and at peace knowing that this will past. As the storm rages on all through the night. I fall on my knees and give it all to Christ. This isn't a storm of nature; it's the storm of life.

BOLD AS LION

Having courage isn't a concept that's easily grasped. It's not for the faint of heart. I fought plenty of battles. I'm gonna fight plenty more. I will keep giving praise until my vocals become sore. But this isn't my strength. It belongs to God, the alpha and omega. Whose knowledge is more precious than any elusive treasure. I'm one with God when I walk in the jungle. Never boast of my talents. I'm blessed when I'm humble. Surround me with nonbelievers and I say, that he's the greatest forever and a day.

WALK THE PLANK

"Walk the plank!" the crowd uttered, with no reasoning behind there vernacular.

"Walk the plank!" the captain yelled, showing his disdain for this person's existence.

"Walk the plank!"

A young stowaway spoke up and asked, "What unjust thing has this man done?"

There was no rebuttal.

"Walk the plank!" They believe the man's afraid. But it's them who should be afraid;

the monster that resides in them will surely be slain.

"Walk the plank!" With each step it brings him closer to his fate. Surrounded by shark-infested waters, they use him as bait.

"Walk the plank!"

With his next step, he plunged into the sea. His dying words, "Forgive them, God. It's because of them I am free."

TAKE HEAVE

When I prayed for peace of mind, you answered. I prayed for someone to love, you answered. I needed a new job, you answered. With me seeing you answering my prayers, I had a thought to pray my enemies felt the same. I had to remember. If I wished that I would become them. Somethings are bigger than your personal feelings.

Lord knows I never wanted this; I never sought this out. I never wanted to say these words. I was content being a single grain of sand in the desert. I fear God more than them. I realized all I went through whether self-inflicted or out of my hands. It was meant to draw me closer to you.

My love was on the brink of death. You nursed her back to health and soon the trifecta will be complete. I'm indebted. I will continue your plans. Thank you for loving me. Now I understand.

LORD KNOWS

Lord knows your struggle. He knows your pain. He knows your greatest accomplishments. He knows your shame. He understands you're human. He's still your rock. He heard your cries when you pleaded them to stop.

The Lord knows you want change. You have to meet him halfway. Tomorrow starts today. Yesterday's a footnote. Lord knows what we're up against; please fill us with hope.

SPECIAL

Look at yourself you're beautiful, talented, in ways that get overlooked. You scratch and claw then you scratch and claw again. You never give up. Your smile is contagious. Your heart's amazing.

Your flaws shine like a beacon. Reminding yourself you're human. It's enlightenment you're seeking. You smile at adversity. You welcome diversity.

Overcome your circumstances. You can persevere. You bow down to no man. It's only God you fear. If you become down on yourself, remember these words I uttered. God is with you, my sisters my brothers.

BLIND FAITH

Though I'm surrounded by darkness, I ask the Lord to guide my steps. Lead me in my darkest hour. I am blind. Give blind faith.

I was fool. I thought I had seen things crystal clear. You discarded the shroud that's covering my face. Giving me blind faith.

I may travel a lonely road. It's you who guides my steps. You spoke and said, "Take heave to my voice and never go astray. Even when you're blind, trust your faith.

STILL WATER RUN DEEP

Embrace your pain, cherish your soul. Give Jesus the burden, he'll carry the load. We see men with huge muscles, doesn't mean they wield great strength. Same goes for those who walk with a bible everywhere they go. Doesn't mean he wields great faith. Exterior means nothing. It's your heart that matters. The Lord knows your thoughts, even the smallest of chatter. Naysayers will be prevalent. Pay them no mind. Soon their world will become desolate. Let God be your strength whenever you're weak. Always keep in mind STILL WATERS RUN DEEP.

WALK ABOUT

Envious stares, snakes hiding within the crack and crevices. Please shed light upon the soulless. As they walk about the earth.

They passed a law to leave infant baby's silent. Then point the finger at hip-hop for promoting violence. Please don't contradict yourself as you walk about this earth.

Keeping us ignorant is their main criteria. Pat that boy on the back; his actions prove he's inferior. As he walks about this earth.

So many want to be a part of something. They tremble at the thought of standing alone. As they walk about this earth.

Big brother watches, dissecting us like mad scientists gone awry. Try and try you never be the most high. As you walk about earth.

Seeing this world become vile and detest makes my soul begin to hurt. I hope even through death my words will walk about this earth.

CELEBRATION

We celebrate the life you lived so valiantly. You walked on water you healed the sick. You changed the heart of men never raising a fist. They hated you for your truth. They bought false accusations against you to make you suffer. You let them crucify you. You could've stopped it. But it was your mission to fulfill the prophecy foretold by the prophets. Our enemies celebrate your death. That's why we celebrate your resurrection.

HUMAN ERROR

BLVD

BEING HUMAN

We seek perfection in so many. Blind to our own imperfections. Think about the kid who's belittled for being different. All he wanted was to be left alone. His cries we ignored. We despise righteousness, we embrace doing wrong. Helping people so everyone can see what you've done. Looking for praise among humans. Help these people but not for recognition. Show them you're being sincere. Why should the rich look down on the poor? Why should the poor envy the rich? Why is this a question that needed to be asked? I know when the masses see this, they're gonna think it's all an illusion. I'm not mad at you. You're just being human.

POEM TO MYSELF

Don't you dare waver. You've come too far to even doubt for one moment. Do not hide your weakness, embrace it. After all you're just human. You sailed treacherous waters. You've scaled mountains filled with hate. You fell down but you got back up. You have a great support system you rely on as a crutch. Never lower standards for acceptance. Remember the only time you truly fail is the moment you give up. It was never an option, so treat as such.

I thought this barbaric mindset died with Hitler. But apparently there are still those among us that want to see the world burn.

Silly me. For some strange reason I thought if we could overcome a global pandemic, it would remind us of how fragile we are as humans. But yet here we are again at the threshold of destruction.

I was pondering how we limit learning black history to a month. If it happened in America, it should be taught yearly in America just like all history.

Please pay me no mind. I'm just thinking out loud.

LOVE YOURSELF

So what, they don't like you. If you never disrespected them, don't go out of your way to make them like you. As humans we're unique and different. We spend so much time trying to prove we're not. We're not robots programmed to the same wavelength. But then again…? Trust me, nobody hates when you're doing bad. When you're on an upward trajectory, they bring up your past. So smile. Be comfortable in your own skin. Love yourself. Be your own best friend.

THE MIRROR

Human beings we're so quick to judge. In your mind you're perfect. In his mind, he's perfect. No man's better than the next. We all have purpose. We'll all answer for our wrongs and none above this. Finger-pointers be leery. Your ways make you weary. Your reflection's vague. You can't see your faults clearly.

WHO AM I?

Am I the person that I strive to be? Does my strength permeate for the world to see. I'm on a path destined to be a freak. An outcast. Is it strange to you I find comfort in that? God is my driving force. And I his conduit. He said harken to me, soon this will all make sense. He's alive, even his enemies acknowledge it's true. Now you know who I am. The question that remains: Who are you?

THE ART OF PEACE

Approach someone with anger, they will react with anger. Approach them with calm demeanor, you'll get the opposite of angry. Violence give's birth to more violence. It's exhausting trying to fight every battle. Don't look at a microcosm of today. Focus on the big picture of tomorrow. Sad but true, hatred passed down like deadly disease that can't be contained. Sometimes a simple hug or it's gonna be OK can work wonders. Everybody won't get along. Respecting the next man will pave a way to peace.

EMOTIONS

Humans oh humans our emotions imprison us. It's our toughest battle. They make us react, regretting our choices. Anger, jealousy, and hatred are the worst of these emotions. That's why our flesh makes us weak, feeble beings. To understand our emotions can't be done through human ways of thinking. We will never master them. But we can learn to keep them under control. Making decisions based on emotions will leave you lost in the wilderness. In a constant loop, always ending up back where you started. When our emotions overwhelm us, we become vulnerable. Struggling to make sense of life itself.

FRIEND I NEVER HAD

Kindness is rare. Loyalty even harder to come by. Is there a friend who tells you the truth about situations you should try to avoid? Or the yes-man who agrees with everything, who says "yeah it's cool, go ahead act a fool." But smiles in the shadows whenever you stumble. Childhood memories of laughter and adolescent decisions. Only to be led astray by society causing more divisive. The more I grow in wisdom, the river grows wider separating us. Stranding us on opposite banks. Leaving us confused, trying to make sense through human eyes. Never fully understanding what has transpired. Or maybe we ignore the clues in our quest to be right. Realizing God is our only friend in this celestial fight.

PRICELESS

You're great in so many ways. Money doesn't define you. You're not perfect. We all know that struggle. You go to work to a job that's not the greatest. It's all for the kids. You wanna see them make it.

That's priceless!

Who cares if friends envy you for changing for the better? The real friends stand by you through inclement weather. They say you'll never be the solution. You're predestined to be the problem. But yet you keep breaking the mold.

That's priceless!

You weren't dealt the best hand. Raised in a broken home. You witness tragedy after tragedy. Life seems glum. You still can overcome. You're just a diamond in the rough.

Whose worth is priceless!

CHAIN REACTION

Life a story that's unwritten. With every decision it manifests words on the page.

Situations can test the human spirit. Emotions can obscure your vision. Our dreams keep us striving. Worrying about your past will destroy your future.

To be conscious is to be positive. To be happy is a choice. To doubt is human nature. To find yourself means looking within.

Holding a grudge will make you lose focus. Teaching children morals is the top priority. Loving them goes without saying.

Time can't be defeated. Understanding purpose will give your life meaning.

STREETS OF BLOOD

As I sit back and watch this world become polluted. Constant prayer to God for positive solution. Evildoers paint the streets red. Molly zombies walk the streets like the night of the living dead.

People see what's happening and turn the other cheek. They blame me for their shame and truth that I speak. It was never my plan to become this person. I take comfort in Jesus while they sleep with serpents.

Good mothers have nightmares of their children dying. While soulless mothers follow an oppressor whose motives are spreading hatred and lying.

So when judgment day comes, you can't say you weren't warned about signs you ignored while in human form. So go ahead scoff and laugh. No structure built by man can withstand his wrath. I would rather stand with God than be still and silent. I refuse to join the ranks of an evil, no-good tyrant.

INTERNAL CONFLICT

Emotions raging, change seems to be on the horizon. You see what needs to be done. The unknown terrifies your thought process. Failure your biggest enemy. Success seems light-years away. In the midst of this, your will strengthens, the perspective is broader. Yet again doubt knocks at the door. Do not answer. For he's the harbinger of defeat. Defeat isn't welcome here.

TIME

Time's so strange. Time can break us. Time can heal us.

Time will always remind us we're human.

When you're at peace with Time, life becomes somewhat easier.

Rest assured all those Times you burnt all those bridges.

There will be a Time you'll have to cross those same bridges at some Time.

We can never get back Time we lost.

We can still make a difference with Time going forward.

Humans think we can overcome Time. Show me one human that has.

I'll wait for it. Like I said Time after Time waits for no man.

LOVER CT.

THE MOTH AND THE FLAME

Why does the moth pursue the flame? A forbidden desire that's unknown to man. It's as though the universe pulls them apart only to bring them closer. The moth can't resist putting his life at risk. The flame calls to his spirit as if telepathic. The feeling intensifies the bond becomes solidified like twins in the mother's womb. Emotions rain down like teardrops of a monsoon. Anticipation leaves the moth weak, longing for more. Humans see this and to us this is strange. We could never comprehend the fate of moth and the flame.

ENDEAVORS OF THE HEART

Have you ever wanted something so bad you find yourself pondering, wondering to the point you can't concentrate? You overthink the words you speak. I wanna be perfect for her. So I pretended to be strong, but for her I am weak. Any moment we share, I'll always cherish. To me she is a goddess. I'm a slave to her will. With no makeup or fancy clothes, she's beautiful still. The sun envy's her glow. I float on cloud nine when I see her message. But yet I feel unworthy because I was born a peasant. I often contemplate of building a spaceship to see different star systems and galaxies. Only stopping to make love on a planet with no gravity. I'm not without sin. I'm flawed beyond measure. This is my heart and all of its endeavors.

WRITINGS ON THE WALL

Your love awakens my creativity. Our spirits speak to one another through telepathy. We are different than most. We're the anomaly. I feel like I've loved twice. Once this lifetime and once in a past life. I tried to stay away. I even act discreet. I daydream of you all day. I call out for you in my sleep. You're the answer to my equation. You hold the map to my heart. I'm your masterpiece and you're my work of art.

THE RAIN

As the rain begin to fall, my heart flutters with expectations of holding you, sheltering you from the deluge. As every raindrop falls, I slip deeper into the abyss of love. The precipitation floods my soul with emotions. Swimming in the attraction that formed between us. As the lightning crackles, fear not, my love. Hold me tighter, we'll face this together. Powerful winds of the storm try to separate our souls. The more it tries the more we grow.

CELESTIAL LOVE

My mind has traveled to the ends of the universe. I found there may be other stars, but you shine the brightest. It may take me light-years to get to you. But when I do, our love will create a supernova. Exploding with passion, showing the universe our love's complete. This will be a beacon for the planets to align. Galaxies far beyond will speak of this bond. That started as a grain of stardust. Now look what it's become.

NO WORDS

You don't have to speak. I can hear everything your heart desires. Such beautiful eyes, they tell a story that's intriguing. Your body language says I'm yours for the taking. My whole being responds with vibes I can't resist. Please never turn it down. I hear you loud and clear. Words are irrelevant when hearts are near.

MOMENTS

The moment when our eyes made first contact, it was different than any moment I can recall. I felt compelled to your aura. All through the day, all I think about is you. In that moment, are you thinking about me too? And when we hug, it puts everything in perspective. Though the moments we have are limited. The effect they leave I will carry the rest of my days. These moments, these feelings I hope they never go away.

IMMACULATE CONNECTION

We never know when loves on the horizon. She lifted me up so I didn't have suffer. In that trice our love was discovered. You're my rock, the one I rely on. I saw you become a woman and I a man. We're a power couple. We're stronger together, the envy of the world. What we have some search their whole life. I'm grateful and blessed to have you as a wife.

FAMILY TREE CIRCLE

THE BEST PART ME

The joy of my life, it's you, my son. You're the reason I work so hard. From birth we shared a bond. When I think about how much I love you, it brings me to tears. Not sad tears but tears of joy. Without you I would be lost. I can recall the first time you walked, the first you talked. I want you to know, I'll fight to be the best thing in your life. You're the apple of my eye my little beam of sunlight. You're all of those things plus more. You'll always be my son. The one who I adore.

MY HERO

She is the definition of strength. Her independence personifies all that's strong in a woman. Working two jobs, she made it seem effortless. The latest attire, she gave us the best. Always keeping it together, even though she was stressed. Me being respectful and having manners are a reflection of her. My back, you have it. When I was wrong, you let me know it. Such a momentous feat, that's what makes you heroic. No man could box you in. Your children came first. They kicked you down but yet you rose like the phoenix. The woman you are, I can't compare to any other. We're your sons and you're most defiantly our mother. My hero.

MEN OF THE HOUR

Good fathers often get overlooked. While deadbeats gets all the attention for all the wrong reasons. Good fathers never want a pat on the back. They may work a lot. Only because they don't want their kids to do without. Their free time is spent bonding, reminding their children they're special. Will walk to the ends of the earth. Words couldn't explain the joy of your birth. This isn't just for blood fathers. This is also for men who take in kids who are not of their own. They still raise them like they were until the day they're grown. We all know any fool can make a child. But it takes a real man to raise one. So good fathers stick your chest out like you couldn't be prouder. Hats off to you, men of the hour.

FOR THE MOTHERS

Mothers are the backbone of society. When we see greatness in someone, it's usually because of their mom. Who works her fingers to the bone so her kids can eat. And keeps a roof over their head, giving them a stable place to sleep. When so many fathers turn coward and run away, moms are the constant willing to stay. A moment of silence for the mothers not here today............................. You give birth. You nurture. You discipline. You give us life lessons. I'm in awe of these mothers. You're truly a blessing.

BLOOD BRUTHAS

My brother from the same mother. Though we're seven years apart. I idealized you right from the start. Like for instance when I wore your outfit to school. I ran all the way trying to beat you home. But you were already there. You was so hot! We almost fought until Moms made us stop. That day you called and you was in jail. I cried. Damn right I cried. Y'all don't understand that's my brutha. If you got a problem with my brutha. You got a problem with me. Go ask me Ms. Shirley, I bet she'll agree. Not too many can say their brutha's their best friend. When we get together, we always laugh and joke. We also grown have men-deep conversations. Telling me if I ascend the whole family will make it. My blood Brutha.

MY FAMILY

Family means the world to me. Years could never change my love for you.

Tragedy strikes again and again. But my love for you bubbles with hope.

This pain makes me weary. My tears stream down like a waterfall.

I feel confused, my sorrow can't be hidden. Tomorrow's not promised, we never have a clue.

Childhood stories of friendship and family ties, I will keep them sacred.

I love you all even if it's been ten years or ten minutes since we crossed paths.

My family, my world

HEAVEN OR
HELL WAY

TEMPTATION

Satan – Why do you believe in something that's not even real?

Me – If he's not real, why do you spend so much time trying to convince people otherwise?

Satan – Join me and I will give you the world and immortality.

Me – I don't want this world. It belongs to you.

Satan – I will turn your family and closest friends against you. You will never succeed.

Me – It's OK I will still love them and treat them with the utmost respect. They've been deceived by your lies and tricks.

Satan – Who do you think you are? Dr. King?

Me – Who do think you are? God?

Satan – Look at yourself. You're poor and you're black. You need me to overcome.

Me – Yes, I'm poor and black. Jesus will help me endure you and this corrupt world.

Satan – They will never accept you.

Me – It was never about being accepted. It's about obeying God and having courage against all odds.

SPIRIT VS FLESH

Flesh – Let's go indulge like we used to do. Live like it's no tomorrow.

Spirit – it sounds fun and all. But he's an adult with children and responsibilities. He has to be conscious about his decisions.

Flesh – Conscious! The world thinks he's just another dumb nigga. Enlighten them, show them what you've seen. Teach them your knowledge.

Spirit – Only arrogant fools jump to show their knowledge in hopes of gaining clout amongst the masses. A wise man waits for perfect timing.

Flesh – Well, well, Mr. Know-it-all. Everyone thinks he's weak. They think they can say and do whatever they want. Release your anger. They don't deserve your kindness.

Spirit – Remember this. You can't control what they do or say. But you can control how you react to it. Vengeance isn't yours.

Flesh – I will never give up. I'll fight you until eternity.

Spirit – Speak for yourself. You will eventually fade away. And I will rest with my Lord for eternity.

A MOMENT TO REFLECT

Our time on earth, as we all know, is short-lived. Like the leaves in fall. It withers away. But our memories are like spring. Bringing life, giving us beautiful clarity of colors that rejuvenate us. Just imagine if we lived forever on this earth. We would watch everyone we love perish over and over again. Appreciate the ones who genuinely love. Keep their memories close to your heart. Nobody can ever take that away. This life serves as a pass for eternity. An unpredictable journey that we must all take. For those that went before us, may your soul rest in heavenly sleep. May God watch over their family, giving them comfort and peace.

LOST LETTERS

HWY

SOCIETY

Dear Society,

I been feeling really hurt. So much madness has happened this year. I've seen unarmed black men be killed. People protesting some rioting. I don't side with violence or revenge. But you can't keep bullying someone and expect them not to lash out. We want justice. Can't you see you're like the parent that paid no attention to us because we're different. We tell you that people mean to cause us harm. You just ignore us, trying to make us feel like it's our fault. Why do you feel like we're so different? The only thing that's different is the exterior. But in the mist of this tragedy, I've seen people from all walks of life and race coming together. It's not just in America but all over the world protesting, standing up against injustice. Truly a beautiful sight. For all those who have love and compassion in their hearts, my hat goes off to you. This country needs that. I get it no matter what you do, some are always gonna have hate in their hearts. As long as you treat me with respect, I'll give you the same and vice versa. At the end of the day, that's all we can ask for. Before I go, America can I ask a hypothetical question? What if our planet was under attack from aliens. Do you think they would see us as the human race? Or view the color of our skin and say we're different? Think about it?

Sincerely yours,
Mr. Nobody

AMERICA

Dear America,

Sense my birth you've always been there for me. When I was an adolescent, you told me you love me. You said I'm lucky to have you. So I loved you so. Early on in our relationship, you always made me feel like I wasn't good enough. So I rebelled. As the adolescent stage passed, I saw a change in my love. Or maybe I was seduced by the lure of feeling accepted. I became opinionated. You hated me for it. I just wanted to spark the minds for positive change. I'll admit I did a lot things in my past I'm not proud of. I can also say the same about you. I don't wanna play the blame game anymore. Maybe we should start holding ourselves accountable for our actions. Start talking about what bothers us. And not become so defensive when we don't agree. All humans are different. We're not going to agree all the time. But we must be conscious of respecting others. At the end of the day if we don't have that, then all will be lost. Every single time we seem to have a breakthrough, here come separatists keeping us doubting things will ever change. I'm gonna stay optimistic about our future for children so they won't make the same mistakes as we did.

Sincerely yours,
Mr. Nobody

STREETZ

Dear Streetz,

I've watched you destroy generation after generation. You seduce our youth. Promising them fast money, expensive cars, and all the things under the sun. You always make good on your promise. But you never tell them that you always come back to collect. Whether incarceration or in death or a lifelong drug addiction. Some abandon their offspring in hopes of gaining your attention. My momma warned me about you. But I didn't listen; I had to see for myself. You used me and when you were done, you moved on to the next. I bet you revel when you hear the saying: "The streetz is my momma and my daddy is the county jail." It's just what you want, for them to feel like you're their only hope. But you have solidity. Just smoke and mirrors and a lifetime of heartache for those who get caught in your wake.

Sincerely yours
Mr. Nobody

FATHER FIGURE

Dear son,

I know I could never take the place of your dad.

But I'm always here for you no matter what. I know you think I can be hard on you. It's only because I wanna see you grow into a great man. You have so much potential. I've been in your life since you was seven. I watched you grow into a young man. Heck, you're even taller than me now. I just wanted you to know I love you with all my heart. Don't ever hold back to address the way you feel. I will always be your father figure, your friend, the person that goes above and beyond so you will never have to do without. But most of all, I love you!

Sincerely yours,
Your Father Figure